ICE HOCKEY

THE STORY OF CANADIANS IN THE OLYMPIC WINTER GAMES

Written by Blaine Wiseman

Published by Weigl Educational Publishers Limited
6325 10 Street SE
Calgary, Alberta
T2H 2Z9

www.weigl.com

Library and Archives Canada Cataloguing in Publication data available upon request.
Fax 403-233-7769 for the attention of the Publishing Records department.

ISBN 978-1-55388-944-1 (hard cover)
ISBN 978-1-55388-953-3 (soft cover)

Printed in the United States of America
1 2 3 4 5 6 7 8 9 0 13 12 11 10 09

Editor: Heather C. Hudak
Design: Terry Paulhus

Weigl acknowledges Getty Images as its primary image supplier for this title.

We gratefully acknowledge the financial support of the Government of Canada through the Book Publishing Industry Development Program (BPIDP) for our publishing activities.

Contents

What are the Olympic Winter Games?

The Olympic Games began more than 2,000 years ago in the town of Olympia in Ancient Greece. The Olympics were held every four years in August or September and were a showcase of **amateur** athletic talent. The games continued until 393 AD, when they were stopped by the Roman emperor.

The Olympics were not held again for more than 1,500 years. In 1896, the first modern Olympics took place in Athens, Greece. The Games were the idea of Baron Pierre de Coubertin of France. Though these Games did not feature any winter sports, in later years, sports such as ice skating and ice hockey were played at the Olympics.

In 1924, the first Olympic Winter Games were held at Chamonix, France. The Games featured 16 nations, including Canada, the United States, Finland, France, and Norway. There were 258 athletes competing in 16 events, which included skiing, ice hockey, and speed skating. The Canadian men's ice hockey team, the Toronto Granites, won all five of its games, and outscored its opponents by a combined score of 110 to 3.

Today, Olympic ice hockey features both men's and women's competitions and is one of the most popular sports featured in the Olympics. Nations such as Canada, the United States, Russia, Sweden, Switzerland, and Kazakhstan are well-known for their skill on the rink.

TOP 10 MEDAL-WINNING COUNTRIES

COUNTRY	MEDALS
Norway	280
United States	216
USSR	194
Austria	185
Germany	158
Finland	151
Canada	119
Sweden	118
Switzerland	118
Democratic Republic of Germany	110

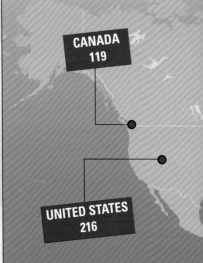

CANADA 119

UNITED STATES 216

CANADIAN TIDBIT Vancouver will be the third Canadian city to host the Olympic Games. Montreal hosted the Summer Games in 1976, and Calgary hosted the Winter Games in 1988.

Winter Olympic Sports

Currently, there are seven Olympic winter sports, with a total of 15 **disciplines**. All 15 disciplines are listed here. In addition, there are five Paralympic sports. These are alpine skiing, cross-country skiing, **biathlon**, ice sledge hockey, and wheelchair curling.

Alpine Skiing

Biathlon

Bobsleigh

Cross-Country Skiing

Curling

Figure Skating

Freestyle Skiing

Ice Hockey

Luge

Nordic Combined

Short Track Speed Skating

Skeleton

Ski Jumping

Snowboarding

Speed Skating

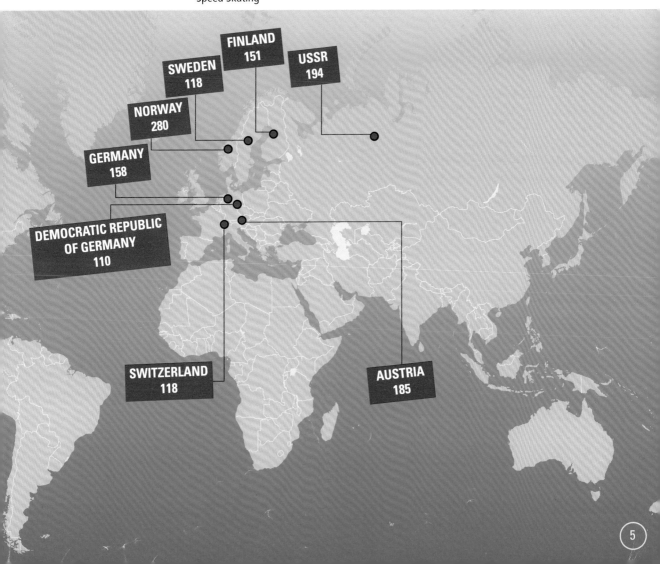

FINLAND 151

SWEDEN 118

USSR 194

NORWAY 280

GERMANY 158

DEMOCRATIC REPUBLIC OF GERMANY 110

SWITZERLAND 118

AUSTRIA 185

Canadian Olympic Ice Hockey

Canada dominated the early Winter Olympics in ice hockey, winning gold medals in 1920, 1924, 1928, and 1932. The first time the Canadian ice hockey team failed to win the gold medal was at the 1936 Olympics in Germany. The team finished in second place to Great Britain. Though Canada had lost the gold medal, 10 of Great Britain's 12 players lived in Canada at the time.

The Winter Olympics were not played during World War II, so the next games were held in 1948. Canada reclaimed its place at the top of the ice hockey world. Although Canada won the gold medal, it finished the tournament with the same record as the team from **Czechoslovakia**. Canada was awarded gold because it had scored two more goals during the tournament than the Czechoslovakians.

At the following Winter Olympics, in 1952, the Edmonton Mercurys won Canada's last ice hockey gold medal of the 20th century. In seven Winter Olympics, Canada had won six gold medals and one silver.

For the next 50 years, Olympic ice hockey was dominated by the Soviet Union. This new powerhouse of hockey created one of the biggest rivalries in sports. Canada and the Soviet Union played some of the greatest hockey games and tournaments in history through the 1960s, 1970s, and 1980s.

The unbeatable Toronto Granites were made up of former World War I servicemen.

In 1924, The Toronto Granites won the gold medal with a 6 to 1 victory over the United States.

In 1998 in Nagano, Japan, women and **professional** athletes were allowed to compete in Olympic ice hockey for the first time. The Canadian women's team featured some of the best female hockey players in the world, including Hayley Wickenheiser, Danielle Goyette, and Geraldine Heaney. The team won the silver medal after losing to the United States in the gold medal final. The men's team featured hockey legends such as Wayne Gretzky, Ray Bourque, and Patrick Roy. The team finished in fourth place, failing to win a medal.

Canada would regain glory at the following Winter Olympics, in 2002. It had been 50 years since Canada had won an Olympic gold medal in hockey. In Salt Lake City, the Canadian women's team beat the American team 3 to 2 in the gold medal final. This was Canada's first Olympic women's hockey gold medal. The Canadian men's team also met the Americans in the gold medal final. Canada won the game by a score of 5 to 2. The 2002 Winter Olympics put Canada back at the top of the hockey world.

At the 2002 Olympics, Canada beat the United States to win its first hockey gold medal in 50 years.

🍁 **CANADIAN TIDBIT** The ice maintenance manager at the 2002 Olympic Games was Canadian, and he placed a loonie under the ice in the centre ice **faceoff** dot. Many people believe that the loonie brought Canada's teams good luck. The loonie is on display at the Hockey Hall of Fame in Toronto.

All the Right Equipment

Ice hockey is a fast, physically demanding sport that requires special equipment to help keep players competitive and safe. Since people first began playing hockey more than 100 years ago, there have been many changes to hockey equipment.

An important piece of equipment used in hockey is the puck. In the 19th century, it was common for players to use rocks, lumps of coal, frozen potatoes, or frozen horse **manure** as hockey pucks. In the 1880s, players began using a soft ball of rubber. Over time, players learned that a disk would slide better along the ice because it would not bounce like a ball. Today's hockey pucks are solid, black rubber disks. A standard puck is 2.54 centimetres thick, 7.62 centimetres in diameter, and weighs about 143 grams.

Hockey sticks are used to move the puck around the ice. For the first half of the 20th century, professional players used wooden sticks that were about 152 centimetres long with a flat blade at the end. In the 1950s, Stan Mikita used a stick with a broken blade to shoot a puck. The puck flew through the air in a different direction than Mikita intended. He then decided to begin curving the blade so he could shoot the puck in different directions, fooling the goaltender. Today, most players today use a curved stick. Though some sticks are still made from wood, other materials, such as fibreglass, carbon fibre, aluminum, graphite, and foam are common today. These materials give sticks greater strength and flexibility and make them a lighter weight.

At first, hockey sticks were made from a curved piece of wood. Today, they are made from more lightweight materials.

As recently as the 1990s, some professional hockey players did not wear helmets. Today, helmets are mandatory in the Olympics. Head injuries are a serious hazard when playing hockey, and today's helmets are a lighter weight and more protective than ever before.

Hockey skates have changed a great deal over the years. In the past, skates were heavy, leather boots with large metal pieces that held the blade to the boot. These skates had very little padding. Today's skates are made of more solid materials, protecting players from damage caused by pucks that travel at speeds of more than 100 kilometres per hour.

Based on cricket pads, modern goalie pads were invented by Emil Kenesky in 1924.

With players able to shoot the puck at faster speeds than ever before, goaltending equipment must offer protection as well as mobility. Goalie pads are made of highly protective, lightweight materials that allow goalies to move quickly around the net, while stopping pucks that can break bones without padding.

🍁 **CANADIAN TIDBIT** Goalie masks became popular when Jacques Plante's nose was shattered by a puck in 1959. After receiving seven stitches, a mask-wearing Plante returned to the ice to finish the game for the Montreal Canadiens. Before he began wearing masks, Plante had received more than 200 stitches to mend wounds from pucks.

Qualifying to Compete

Team captain Mario Lemieux led Canada to its gold medal win at the 2002 Winter Olympics.

In most Olympic sports, only amateur athletes are allowed to participate. However, in 1998, the International Olympic Committee (IOC) decided to allow professional ice hockey players to compete in the Olympics. Players for each country are chosen by the team's coaches and management. Some teams hold **tryouts**, while others **scout** players in various competitions. Players are chosen based on many factors, including their skill, speed, strength, size, and work ethic.

The women's ice hockey event features eight nations competing for medals. The top six teams in the previous Olympics automatically qualify to compete. Other nations must compete in Olympic qualifying tournaments for the remaining two spots. The top nine finishers from the previous Olympics qualify automatically to compete in the Olympic men's ice hockey event. Other teams compete in qualifying tournaments for the remaining three positions.

Both the men's and women's Olympic ice hockey tournaments follow the same format. There is a preliminary round followed

Canadian hockey fans are very enthusiastic about cheering on their team.

Canadian hockey fans have travelled to Olympic sites all over the world to cheer on their team.

by a playoff round and, finally, a medal round. The women's tournament features 20 games. Teams are split into two groups for the preliminary round. The top two teams from each group move on to the semi-finals, with the winners of the semi-finals meeting in the gold medal game.

The men's tournament features 30 games, and teams are split into three groups. The winners of each group, as well as the second-place team with the best record move on to the quarter-finals. The four winners of the quarter-finals advance to the semi-finals. The winning teams from the semi-finals play in the gold medal final. The losers of the semi-final matches meet to determine the bronze medal winner.

OFFICIALS

Officials must be familiar with all of the rules of hockey so that they can do an effective and fair job. In international ice hockey competitions, there is one referee and two linesmen on the ice for each game. These officials wear striped, black-and-white uniforms. If they see a player breaking the rules or the play must be stopped, they blow a whistle. Referees watch for players breaking the rules and penalize players if they feel it is necessary. For example, if a player trips another player, the referee will give the offending player a two-minute penalty for tripping. Linesmen watch

for **infractions** that do not result in a penalty. For example, if a player clears the puck from his own side of centre ice and it crosses the goal line at the

other end, the linesmen will blow the whistle and make an **icing** call.

Rules of Ice Hockey

Ice hockey is a complex game with many rules of play. Basic rules apply to all levels of hockey, while some rules apply only to certain leagues or competitions.

A team is allowed only six players on the ice at all times. Players attempt to score by shooting the puck into the other team's net. Each hockey game has three periods that are 20 minutes each, for a total of one hour of game play. If a winner has not been determined at the end of the third period, a sudden-victory overtime period will be played. The first team to score during the sudden victory overtime period automatically wins the game. If neither team scores during overtime, a shootout is used to decide the game. Five shooters from each team are chosen to take one shot on the goaltender from the opposing team. If the result is still tied after the first shootout round, another shootout round is played.

Some rules protect players from dangerous acts and keep the competition fair. Players are given two-minute penalties for minor infractions, such as tripping another player, striking another player with a stick, or for using unnecessary roughness on another player. More serious infractions can result in double-minor or major penalties. A double-minor is a four-minute penalty, while a major penalty is five minutes. When players receive a penalty, they must leave the ice for the length of the punishment, and their team plays with one fewer player.

Many hockey fans are familiar with National Hockey League (NHL) rules. However, the Olympics use different

🍁 **CANADIAN TIDBIT** The first official rules of hockey were printed in the *Montreal Gazette* in 1877.

Shootouts feature a one-on-one showdown between the shooter and the goaltender from the opposing team.

rules and regulations that are set by the International Ice Hockey Federation (IIHF). For example, the icing rule used by the IIHF is commonly called "no touch" icing. This means that when a player clears the puck from his own team's side of centre ice and it crosses the goal line at the other end, the play is immediately stopped. In the NHL, play is only stopped if a player from the other team touches the puck first after it has crossed the goal line. "No touch" icing is considered more safe than the icing rule used by the NHL because it stops dangerous collisions as players race to touch the puck first. Another example of a rule that is different between the NHL and IIHF pertains to fighting. In the NHL, fighting results in a five-minute major penalty. In the Olympics, players that fight are ejected from the game and may be suspended for the remainder of the tournament.

The NHL was founded on November 26, 1917.

PERFORMANCE ENHANCING DRUGS

Although the Olympics are a celebration of excellence and sportsmanship, some athletes use performance enhancing drugs to give them an unfair advantage over other athletes. There are many different types of performance enhancing drugs, including steroids. Some make muscles bigger, others help muscles recover more quickly, while some can make athletes feel less pain, giving them more **endurance**. The International Olympic Committee (IOC) takes the use of performance enhancing drugs very seriously.

Regular testing of athletes helps ensure competitors do not use drugs to unnaturally improve their skills. Hockey requires a mixture of strength, speed, and endurance. Many performance enhancing drugs will help an athlete in one of these areas, but hurt them in others. For example, a drug may cause the heart to pump more blood to muscles in the arms, making the athlete physically stronger. This takes blood away from the heart and lungs, giving the athlete less endurance and slower long-term recovery. There are serious mental and physical health problems that arise from using

these drugs, such as sleep problems, sickness, and high blood pressure. Athletes who use steroids for a long time may die early from heart attacks and other problems.

Exploring the Venue

An Olympic hockey venue must be able to hold a large number of spectators.

Olympic events are held in huge, specially built venues around the host city. In some cases, the host city already has venues that are suitable to house an event. This is the case in Vancouver, which has two pre-existing arenas that will be used during the Olympics. These are General Motors Place and the UBC Winter Sports Centre.

Being one of the most popular Winter Olympic sports, hockey attracts thousands of fans to games. Canada Hockey Place can seat more than 18,000 people. Even though there are thousands of seats

CEREMONIES

Two of the most-anticipated and popular events of the Olympics are the opening and closing ceremonies. These events are traditionally held in the largest venue that an Olympic host city can offer. Facilities such as football, baseball, or soccer stadiums are often used for these events. At the 2008 Olympic Games in Beijing, more than 90,000 people attended the opening ceremonies. The ceremonies are spectacular displays that include music, dancing, acrobatic stunts, and fireworks. The theme of the ceremonies usually celebrates the history and culture of the host nation and city. All of the athletes participating in the Olympics march into the stadium during the

ceremonies. The athletes wave their country's flag and celebrate the achievement of competing in the Olympics.

General Motors Place was renamed Canada Hockey Place for the 2010 Olympics.

available for each game, it can be difficult to get Olympic hockey tickets. To obtain a ticket to the gold medal final of the men's hockey event, fans must first win a **lottery**. This gives them the option to buy a ticket that can cost as much as $775.

Since Olympic ice hockey follows IIHF rules, it usually features an ice surface larger than those used in the NHL. IIHF ice is 60 metres long and 30 metres wide. However, the 2010 tournaments will be held on North American-sized ice, which is 60 metres long but only 26 metres wide. This is because the venue was originally built for NHL and university hockey games, which use North American dimensions. While a North American ice surface will be used, international rules will apply to the Olympic tournament.

The ice surface is surrounded by plastic boards and glass to keep the puck in play and to protect spectators. It features two blue lines leading to either team's zone, and goal lines at either end of the ice. Nine faceoff dots are placed in various spots on the surface, including five in the **neutral zone** and two in each team's end. In Olympic ice hockey, the centre red line is used to judge centre ice when a player ices the puck. There is no red line **offside** in international hockey, a rule that has been adopted widely by North American hockey federations and leagues.

🍁 **CANADIAN TIDBIT** The Olympic Stadium in Montreal is one of the most expensive stadiums ever built, costing more than $1.4 billion.

Illustrating Ice Hockey

THE SCOREBOARD

It hangs over the center of the rink and displays information about the game: score, penalties, replays, etc.

Team name

Penalty board

Number of penalized player

Penalty duration

Time remaining in the period

Current period

Score

Video replays

THE RINK

Position lines
Located inside and outside the face off circles, they indicate where players must line up for the face off.

Goal lights
There are 2 lights, 1 red and 1 green. The goal judge activates the red light if there is a goal. The green light is linked to the official timer and lights up at the end of each period. If the green light is lit, the red light cannot be lit.

Face off circles and spots
The 5 circles and 9 spots indicate where face offs take place.

Linesmen (2)
They signal icing and offside infractions and stop fights.

Players' bench

Goal judges (2)
Positioned at each end, they make sure that goals are valid.

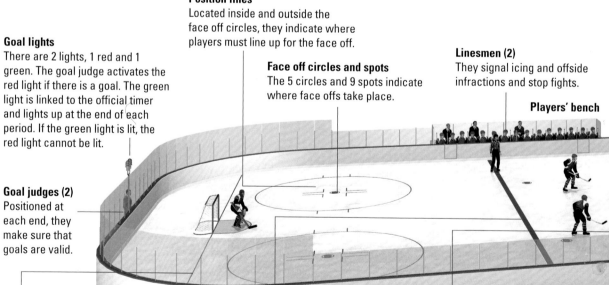

Goal line
The puck must be completely over this line for a goal to count.

Blue lines (2)
They divide the rink into 3 parts: the defensive zone, the attacking zone, and the neutral zone.

Red line
It divides the rink into 2 zones, one for each team.

Announcer
He announces goals scored, penalties, time remaining, etc.

OFFICIALS' SIGNALS

These signals, used by the referees and linesmen, indicate a penalty or infraction of the rules. The game continues until the penalized team touches the puck. There are many penalties in hockey, most of which result in the player or players involved being taken out from the game for between 2 and 10 minutes. Some serious infractions lead to game misconduct penalties or suspensions lasting several games. The penalty time is counted in real playing time. Infractions of the rules are usually offsides and icing the puck.

Delayed penalty
The referee signals a penalty and stops the play when a player from the penalized team touches the puck.

Hooking
Hooking another player with the stick, with the intention of making him fall.

Cross checking
A check made on an opposing player with the stick held in both hands.

Slashing
Hitting a player with the stick.

Goal scored

Goal disallowed

Referee
He controls the game, drops the puck for the face off at the beginning of each period, and makes sure that the rules are applied. In case of a dispute, his ruling is final. In the NHL and major leagues, there may be 2 referees.

Coach
He is the strategist and motivator for his team. He decides what position his players will play and when.

Assistant coaches (2)
They assist the coach, one on offense, the other on defense.

SLAPSHOT

The player's stick is not in contact with the puck. He swings his stick back to give the shot power. The slapshot is less accurate than the other shots.

Neutral zone
Both teams must change players within this zone. Various attack and defense strategies are organized in the neutral zone, which is between the 2 blue lines.

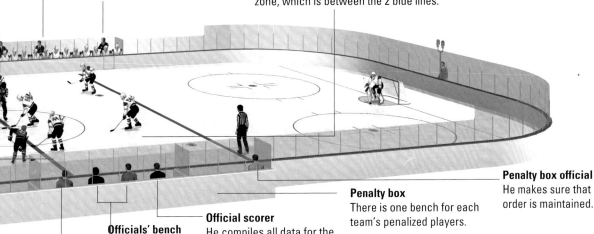

Penalty box official
He makes sure that order is maintained.

Penalty box
There is one bench for each team's penalized players.

Official scorer
He compiles all data for the game: goals, penalties, shots on net, saves, etc.

Officials' bench

Timekeepers (2)
The first is responsible for controlling the clock during stoppages in play. The second times the penalties.

Olympic Legends

OLYMPIC MEDALS WON

1

Joe Sakic

Joe Sakic was born in Burnaby, British Columbia, on July 7, 1969. In the 1987 NHL **draft**, he was picked in the first round, 15th overall, by the Quebec Nordiques.

When the Nordiques moved to Colorado and became known as the Avalanche for the 1995 to 1996 season, Sakic was the team captain and led the team to its first-ever Stanley Cup Championship. He also won the Conn Smythe award as the most valuable player in the playoffs. Sakic has won many other awards in his NHL career, including a second Stanley Cup, the Hart Trophy and Lester B. Pearson awards as league MVP, and the Lady Byng Award. Sakic's strong play for Canada in international tournaments has earned him the nickname "Captain Canada." He has won gold medals at the 1988 World Junior Championship, the 1994 World Championship, and the 2004 World Cup of Hockey. As an assistant captain at the 2002 Winter Olympics, Sakic scored two goals and an assist in the gold medal final against the United States. Sakic was named the tournament's MVP. At the 2006 Winter Olympics, Sakic was team captain.

OLYMPIC MEDALS WON

1

Mike Eruzione

In 1980, the U.S. men's hockey team completed one of the greatest **upsets** in Olympic history. The team, made up of college hockey players and amateurs, defeated the favoured Soviet Union in the semi-final in front of a hometown crowd in Lake Placid, New York. The Soviets had dominated Olympic hockey since the 1960s and had defeated the U.S. team by a score of 10 to 3 only a week earlier. With legends such as Vladislav Tretiak, Igor Larionov, and Slava Fetisov, the Soviets were considered the powerhouse of the tournament.

The comeback victory was the result of a twenty-foot **slapshot** that was completed by Mike Eruzione midway through the third period. Eruzione was the captain of the U.S. team, and he retired from hockey one week later because he wanted to "go out on top." The game, now known as "The Miracle on Ice," is still considered one of the greatest moments in hockey and Olympic history.

Mario Lemieux

Mario Lemieux is considered one of the greatest hockey players in history. During his NHL career, Lemieux led the Pittsburgh Penguins to back-to-back Stanley Cups in 1991 and 1992. In the 1987 Canada Cup tournament, Lemieux, along with his linemate Wayne Gretzky, helped Canada defeat the Soviet Union in a three-game series. In the second time period of the second game of the tournament, Lemieux scored on a pass from Gretzky, advancing Canada to the final game. In the championship game,

Lemieux scored the winning goal on an assist from Gretzky, with only 1:26 remaining in the third period. Mario "the Magnificent" made his impact on the Winter Olympics as team captain for Canada in 2002.

In the final game of the tournament, Lemieux, with his back to the puck, waved his stick as though he was receiving a pass. Instead, he spread his legs, letting the puck slide through to Paul Kariya who scored. Canada won 5 to 2.

FAST FACT

Lemieux is the principal owner and chairman of the Pittsburgh Penguins.

OLYMPIC MEDALS WON

1

Cassie Campbell

As the longest serving captain in Canadian hockey history, Cassie Campbell is one of the most recognizable faces in Canadian hockey. Campbell has won a total of 21 international medals in tournaments such as the Olympics, Four Nations Cup, and the World Women's Hockey Championship.

From 1994 through 1998, Campbell played defence for Canada before switching to forward. Her versatility, skill, and leadership have made her a Canadian hockey legend.

After retiring from hockey in 2006, Campbell became a rinkside reporter for the Canadian Broadcasting Corporation's Hockey Night in Canada. She also does **colour commentary** for the program, becoming the first woman to do this job.

Campbell is a professional speaker who dedicates much of her time to inspiring young girls to follow their dreams. She also participates in, and has created, charity programs to help kids across Canada.

FAST FACT

Campbell is ranked 8th overall with Team Canada's National Women's program.

OLYMPIC MEDALS WON

1   2

WANT MORE?

To learn more about NHL players, visit **www.nhl.com**.

For information about hockey in Canada, check out **www.hockeycanada.ca**.

Olympic Stars

Jarome Iginla

In 2002, Jarome Iginla scored two goals in Canada's 5 to 2 victory over the United States in the Olympic gold medal game. Having represented Canada at various tournaments, including the 2002 and 2006 Olympics, the World Championships, and the World Junior Championships, Iginla is one of the best-known players in Canadian hockey.

As one of the top goal scorers in the NHL, Iginla has won many awards, including the Lester B. Pearson award, the Maurice Richard Trophy as the NHL's leading goal scorer, and the Art Ross Trophy as the leading point scorer. Known as a leader for his work ethic and skill level, Iginla has been an important member of Canada's Olympic teams.

FAST FACT

Iginla donated $2,000 to charity every time he scored a goal during the 2008–2009 regular season.

OLYMPIC MEDALS WON

1

Roberto Luongo

Roberto Luongo is one of the best goaltenders in the world. Continuing the tradition of great Canadian goalies from Quebec, after his heroes Patrick Roy and Martin Brodeur, Luongo won his third consecutive game in April, 2009. Playing in the NHL for the Vancouver Canucks, Luongo's size and speed make it difficult for shooters to score on him.

FAST FACT

In 2008, Luongo was named team captain for the Vancouver Canucks. He is the first goalie to be named captain in the NHL since 1947.

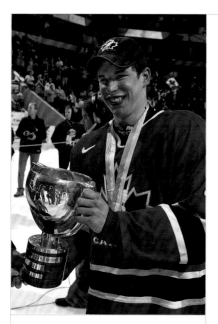

Sidney Crosby

Widely considered the best Canadian hockey player today, Sidney Crosby has been compared to Wayne Gretzky, or "the Great One." Playing for the Pittsburgh Penguins of the NHL, Crosby is one of the smartest, most effective hockey players in the world.

When Sidney was 17 years old, he was the first pick of the 2005 NHL Entry Draft by the Pittsburgh Penguins. He was considered one of the most highly valued draft picks in hockey history.

Sidney began getting hockey awards from a young age, and has played on many winning teams. In 2007, when he was 20 years old, he became the captain of the Pittsburgh Penguins. This made him the youngest player to be made captain in the history of NHL.

FAST FACT

When Crosby was 19, he became the youngest team captain in NHL history.

Hayley Wickenheiser

Hayley Wickenheiser is the best-known female hockey player in the world. She has dominated women's hockey for many years and has even played professionally in men's hockey.

After trying out for the Philadelphia Flyers in 1998 and 1999, Hayley made her professional men's hockey debut in 2003 for Salamat, a professional team in Finland. She now plays for the Calgary Oval X-treme in the National Women's Hockey League (NWHL).

Wickenheiser was the assistant captain for both the 2002 and 2006 Canadian women's Olympic hockey teams and has been named the team captain of the 2010 team. She was awarded MVP honours for both the 2002 and 2006 tournaments. A natural athlete, Wickenheiser played baseball at the 2000 Summer Olympics as well.

FAST FACT

Sports Illustrated named Wickenheiser number 20 of the top 25 toughest athletes in the world.

OLYMPIC MEDALS WON

1   2

WANT MORE?

For up-to-date details about Canadian Olympic hockey, visit **www.ctvolympics. ca/news-centre/newsid=12460.html**.

To learn how to play hockey, visit **www.playsportstv.com/hockey**.

A Day in the Life of an Olympic Athlete

Becoming an Olympic athlete takes a great deal of dedication and **perseverance**. Athletes must concentrate on remaining healthy and maximizing their strength and energy. Eating special foods according to a strict schedule, taking vitamins, waking up early to train and practise, and going to bed at a reasonable hour are important parts of staying in shape for world-class athletes. All athletes have different routines and training regimens. These regimens are suited to that athlete's body and lifestyle.

Eggs are a great source of **protein** and **iron**, and are low in **calories**, making them a popular breakfast choice. A cup of orange juice is a healthy breakfast drink, while coffee can give an athlete some extra energy in the morning. A light lunch, including a sandwich, yogurt, fruit, and juice, is usually a good option. This gives the body the right amount of energy, while it is not too filling. Chicken and pasta are popular dinnertime meals.

Young athletes need to practise a great deal and be very dedicated if they want to become professional hockey players.

Early Mornings

Olympic athletes might wake up at 6:30 a.m. to record their resting **heart rate**. Next, they might stretch or perform yoga while their breakfast is being prepared. The first exercise of the day can happen before 7:00 a.m. Depending on an athlete's sport, the exercise routine can vary. A hockey player might be in the gym lifting weights with his or her legs. After lifting weights for an hour, the athlete may move on to **aerobics** to help with strength and endurance.

6:30 a.m.

Morning Practice

By about 9:30 a.m., athletes are ready to practise their sport. For a hockey player, this means lacing up the skates and hitting the ice. Hockey practice is usually run by a coach. Since teamwork is such an important part of hockey, practice is used to get the team working together. The team practises making certain plays and reacting properly in different situations, as well as skating and endurance exercises. After practice, skaters stretch to keep their muscles loose and avoid injuries. Many athletes use a sauna or an ice bath to help their muscles recover quickly.

9:30 a.m.

Afternoon Nap

At about noon, many athletes choose to take a break. Sleep helps the body and mind recover from stress. After waking up at 2:00 p.m., it is time for lunch and then, more exercise. **Core** exercises help hockey players with stability when opposing players are trying to knock them away from the puck. Speed exercises are also important for hockey players. A common exercise for foot speed is to move the feet through a course on the ground. The course can be as simple as a few hockey sticks laid on the floor.

12:00 p.m.

Dinnertime
6 p.m.

After the afternoon workout, it is dinnertime. Another healthy meal helps athletes recover from the day and prepares their bodies for the next day's training. The evening can be spent relaxing and doing more light stretches. It is important for athletes to rest after a hard day of training so that they can do their challenging routine again the next day.

6:00 p.m.

Olympic Volunteers

Volunteers work tirelessly to make sure the Olympics run smoothly and events begin on time.

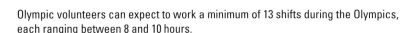

Olympic volunteers can expect to work a minimum of 13 shifts during the Olympics, each ranging between 8 and 10 hours.

Volunteers are an important part of creating an enjoyable Olympic experience for athletes and spectators. Thousands of volunteers help organize and execute the Olympic Games. Olympic volunteers are enthusiastic, committed, and dedicated to helping welcome the world to the host city. Volunteers help prepare for the Olympics in the years leading up to the events.

Before the Olympics begin, many countries send representatives to the host city to view event venues and plans. Olympic volunteers help make the representatives' stay enjoyable.

🍁 **CANADIAN TIDBIT** About 25,000 volunteers are helping with the Olympics in Vancouver. They are helping to make sure the games are a memorable, enjoyable experience for athletes, judges, spectators, and officials from all over the world.

From meeting these representatives at the airport, showing them around the city and the surrounding areas, and providing accommodations and transportation, volunteers make life easier for visitors to the host city.

During the Olympics, volunteers help in many different areas. During the opening, closing, and medal ceremonies, volunteers help prepare costumes, props, and performers for the events. Editorial volunteers help by preparing written materials for use in promoting events and on the official website of the Olympics. Food and beverage volunteers provide catering services to athletes, judges, officials, spectators, and media.

Some volunteers get a chance to view events and work with competitors. Anti-doping volunteers notify athletes when they have been selected for drug testing. These volunteers explain the process to the athletes and escort them to the drug-testing facility. Other volunteers get to be involved with the sporting events by helping to maintain the venues and the fields of play, providing medical assistance to athletes, transporting athletes to events, and helping with the set-up and effective running of events.

Organizers of the torch relay carry a backup flame of the original flame in case the Olympic torch goes out.

Torch Relay

One of the most anticipated events of each Olympics is the torch relay. The torch is lit during a ritual in Olympia, Greece, before it is flown to the host nation. The torch is then carried along a route across the country until it reaches the host city during the opening ceremonies. The torch relay for 2010 covers 45,000 kilometres over 106 days. The relay will begin in Victoria before moving through communities in all 10 Canadian provinces and three territories. About 12,000 volunteers will be chosen to carry the torch across Canada. Other volunteers help drive and maintain the vehicles that accompany the torch on its journey.

What are the Paralympics?

First held in 1960, the Paralympic Games are a sports competition for disabled competitors. Like the Olympics, the Paralympics celebrate the athletic achievements of its competitors. The Paralympics are held in the same year and city as the Olympics. Many sports appear in both the Paralympics and the Olympics, such as swimming, nordic skiing, and alpine skiing. The Paralympics also feature wheelchair basketball, **goalball**, and ice sledge hockey. The first Winter Paralympic Games were held in 1976.

Athletes competing at the Paralympics are classified by disability in six categories, including **amputee**, **cerebral palsy**, **visual impairment**, **spinal cord** injuries, **intellectual disability**, and a group for other disabilities. These classifications allow athletes to compete in a fair and equal basis in each event. Goalball, for example, is a sport for the visually impaired, and not for amputees.

Round poles with bike handles were originally used as sledge hockey sticks.

Just like regular hockey, sledge hockey follows the rules of the International Ice Hockey Federation (IIHF).

Ice sledge hockey is a sport for athletes with lower body disabilities. It was invented in Sweden in the early 1960s by hockey players who wanted to keep playing the sport even though they were disabled. Most ice sledge hockey rules are the same as those used to play ice hockey. The equipment, however, is different.

Ice sledge hockey players use a type of sled instead of hockey skates. These sleds, or sledges, have two blades on the bottom so that the puck can pass underneath. Ice sledge hockey players push themselves along the ice using two small hockey sticks. The sticks have a spike on one end and a blade on the other. Players dig the spike into the ice to push themselves forward. They use the blade to control the puck, similar to a hockey stick.

The length of the sled frame varies depending on the player's size.

Each team has six members on the ice at one time. This includes five players and one goaltender. The objective of the game is to put the puck in the other team's net. Ice sledge hockey is a very fast, physical sport. Full body contact is allowed, meaning players can crash into each other at high speeds. Players must wear protective equipment, including helmets and pads. Since joining the Paralympics in 1994, ice sledge hockey has become one of the most popular sports.

Canada has enjoyed success in Paralympic ice sledge hockey competitions. In four competitions, Canada has won three medals, including bronze in 1994, silver in 1998, and a gold medal in 2006. In 2010, women will be able to take part in ice sledge hockey for the first time at the Paralympics.

The sledge under the sled frame is raised high enough to let the puck pass underneath.

Olympics and the Environment

Hosting so many people in one city can be costly to the environment. Host cities often build new venues and roads to accommodate the Games. For example, a great deal of transportation is needed to support construction projects, planning for the games, and to move the athletes, participants, volunteers, media, and spectators around the host city and its surrounding areas. This transportation causes pollution.

In recent years, the IOC and Olympic host cities have been working to make the Olympics more green. With their beautiful surroundings, including the Pacific Ocean to the West and the Rocky Mountains to the East, Vancouver and Whistler have taken many steps to protect the environment.

As host city of the 2010 Winter Olympics, Vancouver is taking measures to reduce harmful effects to the environment.

WHISTLER SLIDING CENTRE

At the Whistler Sliding Centre, home to the bobsleigh, luge, and skeleton events, an ice plant is used to keep the ice frozen. The heat waste from this plant is used to heat other buildings in the area. All wood waste from the Whistler sites will be chipped, composted, and reused on the same site.

LIL'WAT ABORIGINAL NATION

Working with the Lil'wat Aboriginal Nation, builders of the Olympic cross-country ski trails created venues that could be used long after the Olympics. About 50 kilometres of trails have been built that can be used by cross-country skiers and hikers of all skill levels.

VANCOUVER LIGHTING AND HEATING SYSTEMS

Venues in Whistler and Vancouver have been equipped with efficient lighting and heating systems. These systems reduce the amount of **greenhouse gases** released into the atmosphere during the Olympics.

GREENHOUSE GASES

Half of the organizing committee's vehicles are either **hybrid** or equipped with fuel management technology. These vehicles emit less greenhouse gases than other vehicles. As well, venues have been made accessible to users of transit, and many event tickets include transit tickets to promote mass transportation at the games.

VANCOUVER CONVENTION AND EXHIBITION CENTRE

The Vancouver Convention and Exhibition Centre uses a seawater heating system. This system uses the surrounding natural resources to make the building a more comfortable place to visit. The centre also houses a fish habitat.

RICHMOND OLYMPIC OVAL

The Richmond Olympic Oval was built with a wooden arced ceiling. The huge amount of wood needed to build the ceiling was reclaimed from forests that have been destroyed by mountain pine beetles. These beetles feed on pine trees, killing them in the process. Using this wood helps stop other, healthy trees from being cut down for construction materials.

🍁 **CANADIAN TIDBIT** The 2010 Games are estimated to cost more than $4 billion, including about $2.5 billion of taxpayer money.

Puck Versus Ball

In the early years of hockey, there were no pucks. Hockey players would move around the ice chasing a ball. Hockey players began using a puck because the flat shape slides better along the ice. Balls bounce around, making them more difficult to control.

What you need

a hockey puck or another
   solid disk
a ball
a sheet of ice or a smooth,
   hard solid disk and sheet
   of plastic

1. Slide the puck around on the sheet or ice or plastic. Notice how the puck moves. Does it bounce when it changes directions?

2. Try bouncing the puck on its edge and on the flat side. How high does the puck bounce?

3. Now, slide the ball on the ice. How does the ball move along the surface? What happens when you change the direction of the ball and when you bounce it on the ice?

4. Compare how the puck and ball behave on the ice. Make a list of similarities and differences between the movements of the puck and the ball. What do you think makes the puck behave differently from the ball?

Further Research

Visit Your Library

Many books and websites provide information on ice hockey. To learn more about ice hockey, borrow books from the library, or surf the Internet.

Most libraries have computers that connect to a database for researching information. If you input a topic, you will be provided with a list of books in the library that contain information on that topic. Nonfiction books are arranged numerically, using their call number. Fiction books are organized alphabetically by the author's last name.

Surf the Web

To learn more about the 2010 Olympics, visit **www.vancouver2010.com.**

Learn more about Canadian hockey by visiting **www.hockeycanada.ca/index.php /ci_id/7158/la_id/1.htm**.

Glossary

aerobics: exercise for the heart and lungs

amateur: an athlete who does not receive money for competing

amputee: a person who has had a body part removed

biathlon: a sport in which athletes combine cross-country skiing and target shooting skills

calories: units of energy, especially in food

cerebral palsy: a condition that typically causes impaired muscle coordination

colour commentary: adding opinions and facts to a sports broadcast

core: the trunk of the body, including the hips and torso

Czechoslovakia: a former country in central Europe, which is now divided into the Czech Republic and Slovakia

disciplines: subdivisions within a sport that require different skills, training, or equipment

draft: a process by which players are chosen to play for different teams

endurance: the ability to continue doing something that is difficult

faceoff: two players attempt to gain possession of the puck, which is dropped between them by the official

goalball: a sport for blind athletes; the ball used makes noise, helping blind athletes locate it

greenhouse gases: gases which trap the Sun's energy in Earth's atmosphere, causing the greenhouse effect

heart rate: the number of times the heart beats in one minute

hybrid: a vehicle that uses a combination of fuels

icing: when players clear the puck from their own end of centre ice across the opposing team's goal line

infractions: acts of breaking the rules

intellectual disability: a disability that hampers the function of the mind

iron: a substance in foods that is good for the blood

lottery: a random draw to determine a winner

manure: animal waste

neutral zone: the area between the 30-centimetre wide parallel lines that run across the ice

offside: breaking the rules when both skates of an attacking player cross an opponent's 30-centimetre wide line before the puck is passed

perseverance: a commitment to doing a task despite challenges that arise in the process

professional: an athlete who is paid to play in a sport

propel: push or cause to move in a particular direction, usually forward

protein: a substance needed by the body to build healthy muscles

scout: to watch an athlete for the purpose of acquiring him or her for a team

slapshot: driving the hockey stick blade with maximum force

spinal cord: a bundle of nerves held inside the spine, connecting almost all parts of the body to the brain

tryouts: a competition between athletes trying to gain a spot on a team

upsets: when a lower-ranked team defeats a favourite

visual impairment: not being able to see well

Index